FROM SEA to SHINING SEA

OREGON

TERRY MILLER SHANNON

Consultants

MELISSA N. MATUSEVICH, PH.D.

Curriculum and Instruction Specialist
Blacksburg, Virginia

ELLEN FADER

Youth Services Coordinator
Multnomah County Library
Portland, Oregon

DONNA MURDOCK

Library Media Specialist
Grove School
Milton Freewater, Oregon

CHILDREN'S PRESS®

A DIVISION OF SCHOLASTIC INC.

New York • Toronto • London • Auckland • Sydney • Mexico City
New Delhi • Hong Kong • Danbury, Connecticut

Oregon is located in the north-western part of the United States. It is bordered by Washington, Idaho, Nevada, California, and the Pacific Ocean.

The photograph on the front cover shows the Portland skyline with Mt. Hood in the background.

Project Editor: Meredith DeSousa
Art Director: Marie O'Neill
Photo Researcher: Marybeth Kavanagh
Design: Robin West, Ox and Company, Inc.
Page 6 map and recipe art: Susan Hunt Yule
All other maps: XNR Productions, Inc.

Library of Congress Cataloging-in-Publication Data

Shannon, Terry Miller, 1951-
     Oregon / Terry Miller Shannon.
       p. cm. — (From sea to shining sea)
     Includes bibliographical references (p.) and index.
     Contents: Introducing the Beaver State—The land of Oregon—Oregon through history—Governing Oregon—The people and places of Oregon—Oregon almanac—Timeline—Gallery of famous Oregonians.
   ISBN 0-516-22397-6
   1. Oregon—Juvenile literature. [1. Oregon.] I. Title. II. Series.

F876.3 .S53 2003
979.5—dc21   2002015136

TABLE of CONTENTS

CHAPTER ONE

INTRODUCING THE BEAVER STATE

Oregonians take time to enjoy the scenic beauty of their state at Crane Prairie Reservoir.

Oregon holds an amazing variety of landscapes. You'll find low hills, rugged mountains, volcanoes, and beaches. Trees tower in Oregon's forests, and cactus grow in the deserts. Tall buildings tower over city landscapes, while crops bask in the sun on Oregon's fertile farmland.

Oregon residents enjoy the state's scenic beauty and diverse landscape through a variety of outdoor activities. Hiking, skiing, fishing, hunting, whitewater rafting, exploring tide pools, bird-watching, camping, and windsurfing are all popular with residents and visitors alike. Often, these activities take place within the state's many parks.

Oregon provides the perfect environment for a variety of wildlife, including the beaver. In fact, Oregon is known as the Beaver State. A plentiful supply of beavers attracted early European explorers to the area, who came to trap beavers in order to sell their fur. So many beavers were killed for the fur trade that they nearly vanished. Today, the beaver population is carefully managed and protected. Sometimes called "nature's engineers," beavers are once again building dams in the state's waterways.

Oregon has always attracted people. In the 1800s, many pioneers suffered great hardships because they wanted to live there. Wagon trains started from Independence, Missouri, and reached Oregon in about six months. Along the way, these settlers endured 2,000 miles (3,219 kilometers) of dangerous river crossings, illness, injuries, hunger, and thirst. As you read this book, you'll discover why these early settlers had "Oregon Fever."

What else comes to mind when you think of Oregon?

- Boating on Crater Lake, the deepest lake in the United States
- Hells Canyon, North America's deepest gorge
- Hikers and climbers making their way to the summit of Mount Hood
- Logging trucks transporting freshly cut trees to sawmills
- Waterfalls along the Columbia River Gorge
- Colorful roses blooming in Portland, nicknamed Rose City
- Wind surfers and lighthouses along the Oregon Coast

You'll find all this and much more in the Beaver State. To learn more about Oregon's rich history and unique attractions, simply turn the page. Welcome to Oregon!

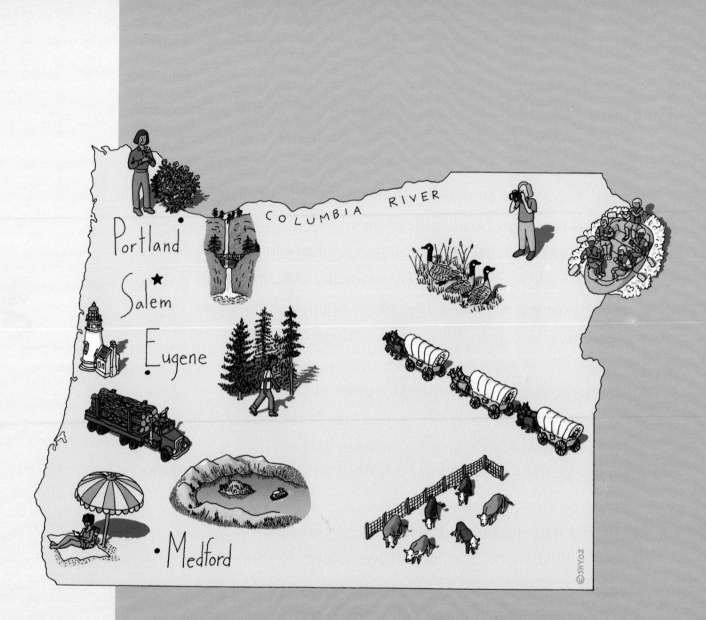

COLUMBIA RIVER

Portland

Salem

Eugene

Medford

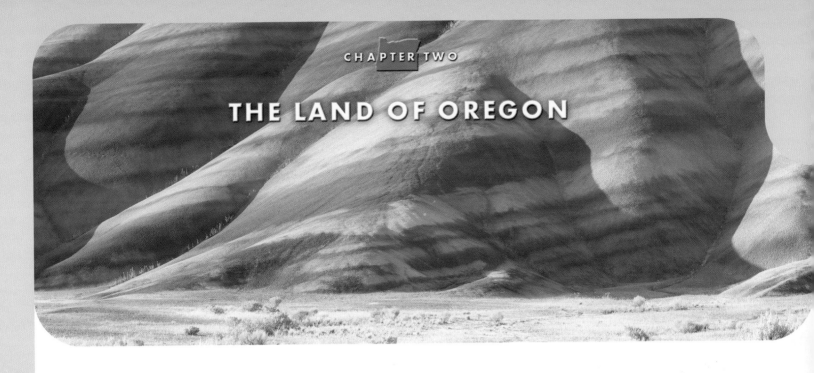

CHAPTER TWO

THE LAND OF OREGON

Oregon is located in the northwestern United States. It nestles up against the Pacific Ocean to the west. Washington is to the north, and Idaho lies to the east. California and Nevada are south of Oregon. Rolling hills, rugged mountains, waterfalls, and sand dunes are all within Oregon's borders, as are rain forests, deserts, plateaus, and fertile valleys. The state covers a total area of 97,131 square miles (251,568 square kilometers). Nine other states are larger.

The mighty Columbia River outlines most of the border between Washington and northern Oregon. The Snake River and Hells Canyon make up more than half of Idaho's eastern border. California and Nevada share mountain and desert along the southern Oregon border.

Millions of years ago, volcanoes, earthquakes, and glaciers (thick sheets of ice) shaped the land we now know as Oregon. Volcanoes erupted, burying plants, animals, and rock in lava, ash, and mud.

The colorful landscape of the Painted Hills can be found at John Day Fossil Beds National Monument in north central Oregon.

Earthquakes broke up the land and pushed it into mountains, forming the western Cascades and the Coast Range. During the ice age, glaciers molded the land by wearing it away and moving earth. When the ice age ended and the glaciers melted, eastern Oregon became warm and dry.

Today, Oregon can be divided into six land regions. They are the Coast Range, the Willamette Valley, the Klamath Mountains, the Cascade Mountains, the Columbia Plateau, and the Basin and Range Region.

COAST RANGE

The Coast Range is a narrow strip of land bordering the Pacific Ocean. There are 362 miles (582 km) of coastline in Oregon. This region has sandy beaches, huge rocks, and mountainous shores. Sand dunes as high as 500 feet (152 meters) tower along the central coast.

Many parts of the Coast Range are heavily forested. Spruce, fir, and other evergreen trees grow there. In some areas, you'll see large bald patches where trees have been clear-cut.

An unusual feature of the Oregon coast is that it is publicly

FIND OUT MORE

"Clear-cutting," which means chopping down all the trees in an area, was once a common method of logging. Today, lumber companies use this method less frequently. New ways to log include replanting and selective logging, which is cutting down only some of the trees in a particular area. How can these methods help protect the forest while producing timber at the same time?

The Oregon coast includes rugged, rocky shorelines and vast sandy beaches.

owned. In many states, private individuals own the beaches and may choose not to allow the public to visit them. In Oregon, the beaches are owned and enjoyed by everyone.

WILLAMETTE VALLEY

The Willamette Valley's rich farmland lies east of the Coast Range along the Willamette River. It stretches from Portland to Eugene. Melting

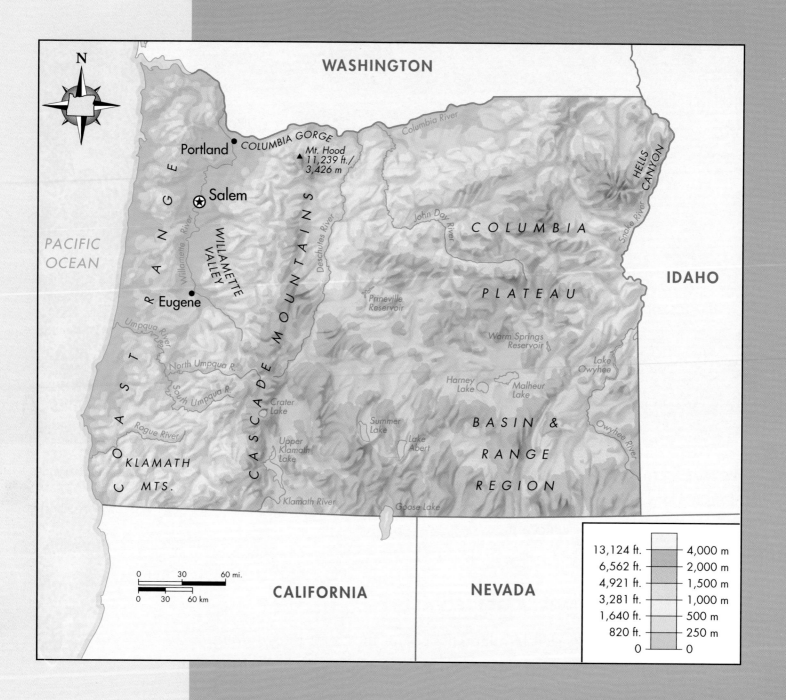

WASHINGTON

N

PACIFIC
OCEAN

Portland
COLUMBIA GORGE
Mt. Hood
11,239 ft./
3,426 m

Columbia River

Salem

WILLAMETTE VALLEY

John Day River

COLUMBIA

PLATEAU

HELLS CANYON

Snake River

IDAHO

COAST RANGE

Willamette River

CASCADE MOUNTAINS

Deschutes River

Eugene

Umpqua River

North Umpqua R.

South Umpqua R.

Prineville Reservoir

Warm Springs Reservoir

Lake Owyhee

Rogue River

Crater Lake

Upper Klamath Lake

Summer Lake

Lake Abert

Harney Lake

Malheur Lake

BASIN &

RANGE

REGION

Owyhee River

KLAMATH

MTS.

Klamath River

Goose Lake

0   30   60 mi.

0   30   60 km

CALIFORNIA

NEVADA

13,124 ft.	4,000 m
6,562 ft.	2,000 m
4,921 ft.	1,500 m
3,281 ft.	1,000 m
1,640 ft.	500 m
820 ft.	250 m
0	0

snow from the Coast Range and the Cascade Mountains feed the Willamette River, which flows north into the Columbia River.

When the last ice age ended, a thick layer of fertile soil was left in the valley. Today, Willamette Valley farmland grows a greater variety of crops than any other region in the United States, including fruits, holly, mint, hops, Christmas trees, irises, lilies, green beans, corn, grass seed, and hazelnuts. Low, hilly, rocky areas are found in the central and northern parts of the valley.

The Willamette Valley is Oregon's most heavily populated area. Almost 60 in every 100 Oregonians live in Portland, Eugene, and Salem. All of these people live in an area occupying little more than one in ten acres (.4 in 4 hectares) of the state.

The Willamette Valley is known for its rich farmland and diverse agricultural products, including flowers, herbs, and wine.

The Klamath Mountains extend from south of the Rogue River into California.

KLAMATH MOUNTAINS

The Klamath Mountains are in Oregon's southwestern corner. They are the western barrier to the Pacific Ocean. Dense forests cover the Klamath Mountains. An interesting feature of this area is Oregon Caves National Monument. The monument includes an old-growth coniferous forest above ground, and a marble cave created over millions of years below ground.

The eastern range of the Klamath Mountains is called the Siskiyou Mountains. Much of the Siskiyou Mountain area is unexplored wilderness. Lumber companies and environmentalists argue over the area's 440,000 acres (178,062 ha) of fir trees. Environmentalists want to preserve the area. Lumber companies believe that logging will not hurt the environment, and that the trees will grow back. Today, fewer and fewer trees are being cut. About one in every ten acres of old-growth forests have remained unlogged. (Old-growth forests are areas of large, old trees.)

EXTRA! EXTRA!

In 1874, Elijah Davidson accidentally discovered the enormous cave we now call Oregon Caves National Monument while he was hunting. Some people say he was chasing his dog, Bruno, who disappeared into the cave opening. Others say he was chasing a bear.

CASCADE MOUNTAINS

The Cascade mountain range stretches from the state's northern boundary to the southern boundary in west central Oregon. The Cascades include Oregon's highest mountain, Mount Hood, at 11,239 feet (3,426 m). The state's second highest peak, 10,497-foot (3,199-m) Mount Jefferson, lies there as well. The average height of the peaks is 6,000 to 8,000 feet (1,828 to 2,438 m). Some of these mountains are inactive volcanoes.

National forests surround the mountains. Some are protected wilderness areas. Other forest areas are logged for timber or used for recreation.

Crater Lake National Park is in the southern Cascades. It is Oregon's only national park, and home to Crater Lake. Crater Lake is the deepest lake in the United States, with a maximum depth of 1,932 feet (589 m). It was formed when a volcano called Mount Mazama erupted about 7,700 years ago. After the explosion, the mountaintop collapsed into a pit 2,000 feet (610 m) deep. Eventually, that pit filled with rain and became beautiful, clear Crater Lake.

Wizard Island is a volcano that rises up from Crater Lake.

COLUMBIA PLATEAU

The Columbia Plateau covers most of eastern Oregon, and also extends into Idaho and Washington. Although there are wheat farms in this

Hells Canyon is a popular place for recreation on the Snake River.

area, much of the region is dry grassland. The Blue Mountains and the Wallowa Mountains are in the eastern part of the Columbia Plateau.

Hells Canyon is in this region. This canyon was carved by the Snake River, on the border between Oregon and Idaho. The average depth of the canyon is 7,900 feet (2,408 m). Hells Canyon is the deepest gorge in North America, and the deepest gorge cut by a river in the world.

EXTRA! EXTRA!

About 20 million years ago, volcanoes in north central and northeastern Oregon erupted floods of basalt rock. The basalt was in liquid form during eruption and hardened when cooled. Because of the volcanic activity that molded the area, basalt is the most common rock type in Oregon. It is usually hard, smooth, and black.

Another spectacular canyon is the Columbia River Gorge east of Portland. It ripples between cliffs filled with waterfalls. One of the most well-known waterfalls is Multnomah Falls—the second highest waterfall in the United States at 620 feet (189 m). The Columbia River Gorge blooms bright with wildflowers from March through April.

The Columbia River cuts through the Cascade Mountains to form the Columbia River Gorge.

BASIN AND RANGE REGION

The Basin and Range Region covers southeastern Oregon. Most of the area is large, lonely desert. There are valleys (or basins) alternating with mountain ranges. River water drains into those basins instead of into the ocean. The 9,670-foot- (2,947-m-) high Steens Mountain is 60 miles (97 km) south of the town of Burns.

LAKES AND RIVERS

Oregon has about 6,000 lakes. The largest natural lake is Upper Klamath Lake, which covers approximately 90,000 acres (36,422 ha). Crater Lake is the deepest lake in the United States, with an average depth of 1,500 feet (457 m). Other lakes include Malheur Lake, Lake Abert, Harney Lake, and Summer Lake. Goose Lake is located on the border of Oregon and California, and part of it lies in each state. The damming of rivers has also created man-made lakes such as Lake Owyhee, Prineville Reservoir, and Warm Springs Reservoir.

Two rivers serve as state boundaries: the Columbia River to the north and the Snake River to the east. The Columbia River is extremely important to the state. Large dams along the Columbia produce most of the electricity for the Northwest. The Columbia also irrigates thousands of acres of farmland, and carries millions of tons of shipping inland each year.

Aside from the Columbia and Snake rivers, Oregon's major rivers include the Deschutes, John Day, Klamath, Owyhee, Rogue, and Umpqua rivers. The Willamette River is Oregon's longest river at 309 miles (497 km). The world's shortest river is in Lincoln City. It is the D River, which is just 100 yards (91 m) long.

Eastern and western Oregon have different climates thanks to the Cascade Mountains. The mountains block moist air from the Pacific Ocean. As a result, the area west of the Cascades gets rain while the east stays drier.

The coast is rainy, with frequent winter storms and summer fogs. Winter storms occasionally bring hurricane-force 100-mile-per-hour (161-kilometer-per-hour) winds and 20-foot (6-m) waves—taller than many one-story houses. Yearly rain averages 60 to 120 inches (152 to 304 centimeters). The average July temperature in the coastal town of Astoria is 60° Fahrenheit (16° Celsius); in January, Astoria's average temperature is 42° F (6° C).

Snow plows are a familiar sight in the Cascade Mountains, where deep snow is a common occurrence.

The Cascade Range and the Blue and Wallowa Mountains get lots of winter rain and snow. The snow feeds rivers and streams when the weather warms. Summers start late, and are hot and sunny.

North central Oregon gets only 10 to 20 inches (25 to 50 cm) of rain per year. The central plateau and southeastern parts of the state have a little less rain; the east receives very little rain. However, there can be lots of winter snow in the higher elevations.

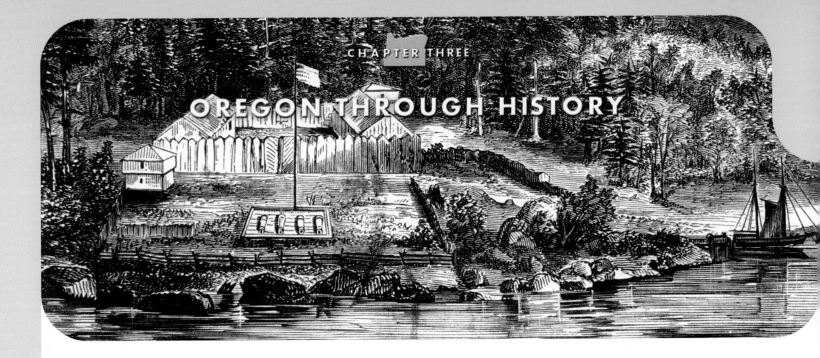

CHAPTER THREE

OREGON THROUGH HISTORY

People have lived in the area we now know as Oregon for 30,000 years. The first people to live there may have traveled from Asia to North America over a land bridge linking the two continents. The largest group probably moved into North America about 14,000 years ago, at the end of the last ice age.

The first natives were Paleo-Indians (*paleo* means "long ago"). They lived along the lakeshores of the Klamath Lakes Basin in what is now southwestern Oregon. The lakes and marshes provided fish and ducks for food. Scientists have found evidence of these early people in central Oregon's Fort Rock Cave. They believe that some of the artifacts date back 13,000 years.

After the ice age, a hot dry spell dried the lakes. Some Native Americans moved north to

Fort Astoria marked the beginning of American settlement in Oregon.

FIND OUT MORE

It is possible that the first people to enter North America hiked over the Bering Land Bridge, a great landmass in the Bering Sea and Chukchi Sea. At that time, sea level may have been 300 feet (91 m) lower than it is now. Today, that land is underwater. Why would the sea be so much lower during the ice age?

Many Native Americans made their home along the Columbia River.

the Columbia River. Others headed to the coast approximately 2,000 to 4,000 years ago. Another group, the Paiute, traveled up through northeastern California, settling in what is now southeast Oregon. Canadian natives moved south to today's Oregon coast.

The lives of the natives differed according to where they lived. Northeastern tribes fished salmon and hunted elk, deer, and mountain sheep. They dug roots called *camas* to eat cooked or raw, and also gathered berries and wild turnips. Southeastern tribes traveled around, following and hunting wild animals. Southern tribes paddled canoes into lakes to harvest yellow water lily seed for food. Their winter homes were pits dug into the ground and roofed with earth. In summer, they lived above ground in homes made from willow tree branches or stems from a water plant called tule. Coastal tribes and those living near the Columbia River used dugout canoes, made by shaping and hollowing out logs. They lived in large wooden homes.

Every year, several native tribes met at a northern area beside the Columbia River (now known as the Dalles) to trade and fish for salmon. Some tribes met in the mountains during huckleberry season. There was also warfare between some of the groups. War victims who weren't killed sometimes became slaves owned by the victorious tribe.

By the time Europeans arrived, tens of thousands of natives lived in the area that would eventually be known as Oregon country. Native American groups included the Paiute in the southeast; the Apache and Navajo at the lower Columbia and parts of the southwest; the Nez Perce and Cayuse in the northeast; and the Modocs and Klamaths in the south. Altogether, there were about 125 tribes speaking more than 50 languages.

Native Americans make their way down the Columbia River in a dugout canoe.

Sir Francis Drake sailed along the Oregon coast in search of the Northwest Passage, a water route connecting the Atlantic and Pacific oceans.

(opposite)
Fort Clatsop was named after a nearby tribe of friendly Native Americans.

EUROPEANS ARRIVE

In the mid 1500s, European explorers came in search of a passage connecting the Atlantic and Pacific oceans. They knew that if such a route existed, it would make trade easier. In 1542, a Spanish ship sailed toward what is now the southern Oregon coast. Juan Rodriguez Cabrillo commanded the ship, but he died before his ship reached the coast. His pilot, Bartolome Ferrelo, guided the ship to the mouth of the Rogue River, but storms kept him from landing.

Other explorers also had difficulty landing. Englishman Sir Francis Drake reached the mouth of the Rogue River in 1579. He left without landing because of what he called "thicke and stinking fogges." In 1602, Spain's Martin de Aguilar was defeated by stormy weather.

Spanish explorer Bruno de Heceta found the mouth of the Columbia River in 1775. His crew was sick with scurvy, so he was unable to travel the river. Around this time, an American fur trader named Robert Gray sailed between the Pacific Northwest and China, selling furs to the Chinese. In 1792, Gray braved the frightening sandbars and entered the river. He named it Columbia's River after his ship, the *Columbia Rediviva*. Gray's discovery of the Columbia was the first American claim to the area.

EXPLORERS BY LAND

The United States was a young, developing country in the early 1800s, and its leader, President Thomas Jefferson, was eager to explore the West. In 1803, Jefferson chose his personal secretary, Meriwether Lewis, and Lewis's friend, William Clark, to head an expedition to this uncharted territory.

Lewis and Clark had several goals. They hoped to find a water route across the continent to aid in travel and trade. The explorers were also expected to report to Jefferson on the plants, animals, and land they discovered. Finally, they wanted to make friends with the natives of that area. All these goals would help to lay a foundation for a United States claim on the territory.

Lewis and Clark kept detailed journals during their trip. Traveling west on the Missouri River, they recorded notes about the land they saw, their interactions with natives, and observations about plants and animals. Fifteen months after leaving St. Louis, Missouri, Lewis and Clark reached the Pacific Ocean at the mouth of the Columbia River. They needed a place to shelter for the winter, and built a small log building, called Fort Clatsop, near today's Astoria. There they hunted game and made salt.

WHO'S WHO IN OREGON?

Sacagawea (c. 1787–1812) was a native woman married to a French-Canadian fur trader named Toussaint Charbonneau. In North Dakota, Lewis and Clark hired Charbonneau and his wife, Sacagawea, to act as interpreters on their trip. Sacagawea proved to be a valuable addition to the traveling party. She helped with route planning because she knew the area. Also, her presence among a group of white men served as a token of peace when meeting Native American tribes.

FIND OUT MORE

Salt was very important in the days before refrigeration. It was used to keep meat from spoiling. In their journal, Lewis and Clark describe what they needed to make salt: ocean water, firewood, and kettles. Describe the steps the salt makers took in order to make salt.

John Jacob Astor worked to establish an outpost in Oregon so that he could become the dominant fur trader in the Northwest.

At last, spring arrived. The group was thrilled to leave the area described in Clark's journal as "wet, cold, and disagreeable." On the way home, Clark discovered the mouth of a river now known as the Willamette. The expedition arrived back east in 1806, with incredible stories to tell of the West's natural resources, including an abundance of fur-bearing animals.

THE FUR TRADE

Lewis and Clark's reports created new interest in fur trading. Two British fur businesses, the North West Company and Hudson's Bay Company, were already established in North America. American fur traders usually sailed out of Boston and sold thousands of furs in China.

In 1810, a wealthy American fur trader named John Jacob Astor sent a ship to the Oregon coast. Another group was sent by land. Astor wanted to start a fur business at the mouth of the Columbia River. He hoped to buy furs from the natives to sell in the Orient.

Astor's land group eventually settled at a spot they named Fort Astoria. This was the first permanent northwest settlement, but it was disrupted by war. During the War of 1812, British warships stopped Astor's supplies from getting to Fort Astoria, and Astor sold the fort to the British in 1813. When the war ended, Astoria was returned to the

Americans. However, the border between Canada (a British territory) and the United States was still in dispute.

Over time, England's Hudson's Bay Company became the most powerful fur-trading company in the Northwest. Their headquarters was at Fort Vancouver at the mouth of the Willamette River. John McLoughlin was a director of the Hudson's Bay Company at Fort Vancouver. When his French-Canadian trappers retired, McLoughlin gave them land on the banks of the Willamette River, even though they were supposed to return to Canada. These French-Canadians were the first settlers in Oregon. McLoughlin also treated the natives with respect. They named him the "White Headed Eagle" for his white hair and piercing eyes.

A fur trapper anxiously awaits a beaver to step into his trap.

Fur traders were not the only ones heading to Oregon. American missionaries were also attracted to the Oregon territory. These missionaries wanted to spread the teachings of Christianity among Native Americans in Oregon. The first missionaries arrived in the Northwest in the 1830s and established settlements in the area. Jason Lee, a Methodist, built a mission near today's Salem in 1834. There were seven missionary settlements in Oregon country by the early 1840s.

In 1843, Marcus and Narcissa Whitman and Henry and Eliza Spalding established missions near today's Walla Walla, Washington, and Lewiston, Idaho. The Whitmans talked to the Nez Perce, Cayuse, and Walla Walla tribes about becoming Christian.

Marcus and Narcissa Whitman traveled farther west by wagon than any American expedition before them.

Over time, however, the missionaries became frustrated with the natives. They didn't agree with many of the natives' ways, such as gambling. The natives were frustrated with the missionaries, too, as they watched church members argue among themselves. Natives began to doubt where the missionaries' ideas came from. One chief said, "Where are these laws from? Are they from God or from the earth? . . . I think they are from the earth, because, from what I know of white men, they do not honor these laws."

In addition, the settlers had unknowingly brought disease to the area. While the settlers themselves were immune to these diseases, whole villages of natives died from measles, smallpox, and other illnesses. The settlers tried to save them and failed. The Cayuse held them responsible and, in 1847, they killed the Whitmans and twelve others in what became known as the Whitman Massacre.

THE OREGON TRAIL

In the early 1840s, pioneers began to travel from their homes in the Midwest to what is now Oregon. People left home for many reasons. Some wanted to leave the crowded Midwest. Jobs were scarce, disease was a problem in some areas, and winters were difficult. Others wanted to seek their fortunes in a new place.

The Organic Act of 1843 motivated many people. Under this act, the United States government offered 640 acres (259 ha) of land to each adult male settler in Oregon country. Each child earned 160 acres (65 ha) more for the family. Because the Northwest did not yet belong to the United States, the government hoped to fill the area with Americans, and then claim the land.

Between 1840 and 1860, 53,000 people headed for Oregon. The route they followed came to be called the Oregon Trail. Most of the wagon-train pioneers were Protestant families. Women were often unenthusiastic about the adventure. It meant leaving home and loved ones to cook, wash, baby-sit, nurse the ill, and give birth under incredible hardship.

The Oregon Trail was the only path available for settlers to cross the treacherous Rocky Mountains.

A woman named Helen M. Carpenter wrote about life on the Oregon Trail: "Although there is not much to cook, the difficulty and inconvenience in doing it amounts to a great deal—so by the time one has squatted around the fire and cooked bread and bacon, and made several dozen trips to and from the wagon—washed the dishes . . . and gotten things ready for an early breakfast, some of the others already have their night caps on—at any rate it is time to go to bed. In respect to women's work, the days are all very much the same—except when we stop . . . then there is washing to be done and light bread to make and all kinds of odd jobs. Some women have very little help about the camp, being obliged to get the wood and water . . . make camp fires, unpack at night and pack up in the morning—and if they are Missourians they have the milking to do if they are fortunate enough to have cows . . ."

Emigrants on the Oregon Trail set up camp each evening around six p.m. to start campfires and cook dinner.

The journey was usually a six-to-eight month trip along a dusty trail. Disease killed many. Attacks from natives were a terrifying possibility. Sometimes children fell beneath wagon wheels and horse hooves. Often people became tired or sick. There was frequently not enough grass for animals to eat. People and livestock drowned in river crossings, while accidents with guns killed some pioneers.

The last part of the journey was very difficult. Wagons had to be drawn up the Blue

Mountains with pulleys and carefully lowered down steep slopes. In 1844, while a group was crossing the raging Columbia Gorge, half of the pioneers' livestock drowned.

When they finally stumbled into Oregon, the settlers were relieved. They were also sometimes disappointed. Although the Willamette Valley was beautiful, the earliest pioneers had taken the best land claims in the area, close to the woods for building but also near open land for planting and grazing. The newcomers had to travel great distances, usually in rainy weather, to find good land claims. Often, new families crowded in with older ones, who shared their food.

One of the area's richest resources was fish. Oregon's fishing industry began in 1823, when settlers caught salmon to sell. Fishing led to the creation of towns as people moved to live where the fishing was good. The commercial fishing industry, especially of salmon, has been an important business throughout Oregon's history.

This salmon cannery near Astoria was bursting with activity in the 1880s.

Oregon City, on the falls of the Willamette River, began as three log cabins built by John McLoughlin during the winter of 1828–1829. In 1832, McLoughlin built a sawmill and a flourmill. Oregon City became the first official town west of the Rockies in 1843, when American settlers voted to start a government with Oregon City as the capital. During the late 1840s and early 1850s, settlers established many new towns, including Portland.

THE ROAD TO STATEHOOD

By 1846, the large number of American settlers in Oregon prompted Great Britain to give up any claims on the region. The international border was marked along the 49th parallel (today's border with Canada). In 1848, Oregon became a United States territory. The Oregon Territory covered what is today Oregon, Washington, Idaho, and western Montana.

In 1849, gold was discovered in California. About one half million people traveled there, hoping for instant wealth. California's Gold Rush tempted many to leave the Oregon area—about two in every three young men headed south. The Gold Rush also gave Oregon settlers a nearby market for farm produce, such as wheat, apples, and vegetables.

The need for new housing in California's Gold Rush Country meant that Oregon could sell timber there, also. The Oregon timber industry began in 1827 at Fort Vancouver, when Hudson's Bay Company workers cut lumber to send to the Sandwich Islands (now Hawaii). By the

Workers operate a busy lumber wharf on the north Pacific coast.

1850s, Oregon had five sawmills. Lumber was sold to China, Australia, and Hawaii.

Washington Territory was split off from Oregon in 1853. On February 14, 1859, with 52,000 residents, Oregon became the thirty-third state. The capital was Oregon City, and John Whiteaker was Oregon's first governor.

GOLD!

In 1852, the discovery of gold in the Rogue Valley drew many fortune-seekers. Gold miners rushed in and settled Jacksonville. They came from all over the United States and from other countries, including

China. Many of the newcomers were rough, tough California miners. One man, Orange Jacobs, said in 1853: "The mines were rich, money was abundant, and gambling rampant."

The United States government offered land to all pioneers without buying it from the native peoples. While some settlers felt that Native Americans were not being treated fairly, others disagreed. Agreements to pay the natives and divide the land, called treaties, were signed by settlers and Native Americans, but the settlers did not pay for the land as agreed. Instead, settlers continued to arrive and take over the natives' land. The new arrivals killed the wild animals, leaving less for natives. They cut down forests for timber, and still more animals died. Trash from the mines was dumped in rivers, killing fish. The Native Americans were starving.

The settlers' greed for precious metals and land caused thirty years of violence between settlers and natives. Fights with Native Americans over land claims resulted in the Rogue River Wars (1851–1856). The natives attacked the settlers, fighting for their homes, their food, and their lives. In 1856, the United States army won the war, leaving Native Americans defeated.

The government tried to solve the problem by establishing a reservation system. A reservation is a piece of land set aside as a place for Native Americans to live. Some Native Americans went calmly to the reservations. Others fought bitterly. Native resistance to reservation life resulted in the 1872 Modoc War and the 1878 Bannock-Paiute War.

The promise of gold attracted many new settlers to the West.

33

Natives headed for reservation life gave up their lands, language, and way of life. Different tribes were forced to live together, even when they were enemies. Children on reservations were forced to speak English and attend strict military-type schools. Since there were few jobs on the reservations, the natives living there were poor. Natives were told to farm even when the land was not farmable.

Oregon reservations were the Siletz, Grand Ronde, Warm Springs, Umatilla, Klamath, and Malheur. Some of the tribes who entered the Siletz Reservation were Tututni, Coos, and Nestuccs. Natives of the Grand Ronde Reservation were a group of eight tribes (including Alfalati, Luckiamute, and Yoncalla tribes) called the Kalapuyan tribes. The Wasco and Northern Paiute went to the Warm Springs Reservation. Tribes of the Umatilla Reservation were the Cayuse, Umatilla, and Walla Walla. Klamath, Modoc, and Yahooskin Band of Snake Indians lived at Klamath Reservation. Paiute Indians moved to the Malheur Reservation.

In 1855, the Nez Perce tribe peacefully moved to a large reservation in northeastern Oregon and present-day Idaho. When miners found gold on reservation land in 1863, some native leaders agreed to accept a much smaller reservation. About one third of the tribe felt this settlement was unfair and moved elsewhere.

WHO'S WHO IN OREGON?

Sarah Winnemucca (1844–1891) was a descendant of Paiute chiefs. By the age of fourteen, she knew five languages. When she was twenty-seven, she became an interpreter for the Bureau of Indian Affairs at Fort McDermit on the Oregon border. She devoted all her efforts to improving the life of the Paiute. Winnemucca became the first Native American woman author when she published her book, *Life Among the Paiutes*.

In an 1877 struggle between land-greedy whites and a group of Nez Perce, the natives were ordered to move to the reservation. Angered, three young warriors killed four local settlers. Six hundred Nez Perce natives tried to escape to safety in Montana or Canada. As the army pursued them, many people on both sides died. A Nez Perce leader, Chief Joseph, gave up. He said, "Hear me, my chiefs! I am tired. My heart is sick and sad. From where the sun now stands I will fight no more forever."

As the tribes were removed, settlers moved into their vacated lands. The settlers filled southern Oregon with farms, ranches, orchards, and logging towns. Gold miners started Gold Beach and Port Orford, on the southern coast, in the 1850s. Gold Beach was named for the gold mixed into the beach sand at the mouth of the Rogue River. A flood washed the beach clean of gold in 1861, but mining up the river continued for years.

Chief Joseph and his people were moved to a reservation in Oklahoma.

EXTRA! EXTRA!

Many Chinese people came to Oregon to seek their fortunes during the Gold Rush. Gin Lin was a Chinese immigrant miner in the Applegate Valley in the 1880s. He was typical of many Chinese miners in that he saved his money and worked hard. In fact, he worked so hard that he eventually owned several gold mines. Many Chinese, however, led difficult lives in Oregon. They lived in terrible conditions and worked hard for poor wages. Most Chinese eventually returned to China.

GROWTH AND CHANGE

In 1844, Tennesseean William Overton wanted to claim land in north-western Oregon. He didn't have the twenty-five cents he needed to file a claim, so he offered his friend, Amos Lovejoy, a half-share if he would pay the fee. Later, Overton sold his share of the land to Francis Pettygrove from Portland, Maine, for $100 worth of goods. This land later became the city of Portland.

By 1845, the town was still without a name. Lovejoy and Pettygrove couldn't decide between Boston (a city in Lovejoy's home state, Massachusetts) and Portland (the largest city in Pettygrove's state, Maine). The two men tossed a coin, and Portland won.

The population of Portland was 821 in 1860, but by 1870, 9,565 people lived there. Trade boomed along the Willamette River. The road south of Portland enabled easy transport of produce and lumber to the ocean. New factories and wharves were built.

Portland was a bustling town in the late 1800s.

Oregon's fishing industry also continued to develop. Abundant salmon was caught in the rivers and the ocean. In 1867, the state's first salmon cannery was built on the Columbia River. Astoria, on Oregon's northern coast, became the center of the fishing industry. However, by 1877, the salmon population was nearly wiped out. Places to raise young salmon, called fish hatcheries, were built to help replenish the scarce salmon.

Along with developing industries came the railroad. The first railroad in Oregon was built in 1862 by the Oregon Steam Navigation Company. It crossed 5 miles (8 km), from Tanner Creek to the head of the Cascades. Next, the Oregon Steam Navigation Company built a 14-mile- (23-km-) long railroad from the Dalles to Celilo. Oregon's railroads eventually ran along the south bank of the Columbia east to the Umatilla River, southeast over the Blue Mountains into Idaho, and from Portland to Sacramento.

On July 1, 1862, President Abraham Lincoln signed the Pacific Railroad Act, approving the building of the first railroad that stretched from the east coast to the west coast—the Transcontinental Railroad. By 1883, you could take a train from Portland to Minnesota. The new railroad system changed the way settlers entered Oregon. A trip that once took as long as six to eight months by wagon could now be completed in a few days.

A rail car makes its way through the Cascade Mountains.

Thanks to the railroad, Oregon's huge Douglas fir trees could now be logged in large amounts and carried east by train. People believed the tremendous forests were endless, so lumber companies stripped the forests of trees. As the 1900s began, the government wanted to be sure that all of Oregon's trees were not cut down. The United States Department of Agriculture (USDA) Forest Service was created in 1905. The Forest Service conserved (protected) public forests by restricting cutting on public lands and limiting how much lumber could be sold.

In 1914, World War I (1914–1918) broke out in Europe. The United States tried to stay out of the war, but that changed in 1917, when German submarines began to attack United States vessels. President Woodrow Wilson declared war on April 6, 1917. More than 44,000 Oregonians served in World War I. Oregon's shipyards grew because of the demand for warships. The state continued to prosper even after the war. The timber industry increased, and the coast town of Coos Bay became the world's largest lumber-shipping port.

Prosperity lasted until 1929, when the stock market crashed. Hard times gripped the nation. Oregon, along with the rest of the United States, suffered through what is known as the Great Depression (1929–1939), a period of national poverty. Many people lost money when the price of stocks fell. They could no longer afford to buy things, which meant factories closed and people lost jobs. Things were even worse in other parts of the country. The Midwest experienced a drought (a long period without rain), and farmers weren't able to grow crops.

WHO'S WHO IN OREGON?

Henry Villard (1835–1900), a German immigrant, became president of the Northern Pacific Railroad in 1881. Under his direction, the railroad's transcontinental line was completed in 1883, connecting Oregon with the East Coast. The railroad drew 30,000 settlers to Oregon.

In the 1930s, many migrant farm workers from the Midwest headed to Oregon to look for work.

Many people moved to Oregon from the Midwest during the Great Depression, hoping to find work.

In order to help people get back to work, President Franklin D. Roosevelt established conservation projects under a program called the New Deal. In Oregon, Roosevelt's Works Progress Administration and the Civilian Conservation Corps hired workers to set up irrigation systems, replant forests, and build dams.

The New Deal resulted in the Bonneville Dam across the Columbia River in 1937. The dam controlled water by pumping it out of a reservoir, or man-made lake, behind the dam. The water could then be used

The Bonneville Dam was one of the largest hydro-electric projects under the New Deal.

to irrigate dry land, or supply it with water. Irrigation enabled farmers to grow potatoes and wheat in dry northeastern Oregon. Dams also helped to prevent flooding and generated electricity.

Although new dams were important to Oregonians, they created problems for salmon. Salmon must swim from the ocean (where they spend most of their lives) up the river to lay eggs. The dams blocked salmon movement, preventing them from reaching their spawning grounds. As a result, the salmon population greatly decreased. Today, fish ladders have been built to allow salmon and other fish to migrate past the dams.

Progress also affected other animals. In 1938, Oregon became the highest producing lumber state in the country. By the 1950s, tree farms started to grow new trees, but loggers removed trees faster than they could be grown. Eventually, logging destroyed the forest home of a bird called the northern spotted owl.

WORLD WAR II

The Great Depression gradually came to an end with the start of World War II (1939–1945). The United States entered the war in 1941, and almost 148,000 Oregonians served in the armed forces. Many other Oregonians helped on the home front, building ships for American troops. Shipbuilding boomed again, and Portland grew to be one of the country's major shipbuilding cities.

Aluminum was also in high demand for war supplies. The manufacture of aluminum required large amounts of cheap electricity, which Columbia River dams provided. Aluminum became an important industry in Oregon.

During the war, many people across the country were suspicious of Japanese Americans because the United States was fighting against Japan. Some United States leaders feared that Japanese Americans might be spies. In 1942, President Franklin Roosevelt ordered Americans of

EXTRA! EXTRA!

When the northern spotted owl was listed as a threatened species in the 1990s, the government closed many forests to logging. Environmentalists believe the spotted owl is a symbol of healthy forests—if the spotted owl is in danger, so are our forests. However, loggers believe that the forest closures are costing people lumber and jobs. Because the government owns more than half of Oregon's land, much of the state's logging has been stopped.

WHAT'S IN A NAME?

The names of many places in Oregon have interesting origins.

Name	Comes From or Means
Appaloosa horse	Named for the Palouse Hills near the Nez Perce tribe, who were expert horse breeders
Cape Ferrelo	Named for Spanish ship captain Bartolome Ferrelo
Douglas fir	Named for David Douglas, 19th century Scottish plant scientist
Chinook salmon	Named for the Chinook Native Americans
Astoria	Named for John Jacob Astor, wealthy owner of a fur-trading company, whose men started the settlement
Klamath Lake	Named for the Klamath tribe
Salem	Arabic *salaam* and Hebrew *shalom*, meaning "peace"

Japanese descent to be moved from their homes. Across the country, 117,000 Japanese Americans were locked up in internment camps.

In Oregon, Japanese Americans were sent to an internment camp in the eastern part of the state. The camp was surrounded by barbed-wire fences and patrolled by soldiers. In Portland, 3,800 Japanese Americans were crowded into a fairground livestock barn divided into apartments. Although World War II was also fought against Italy and Germany, only Japanese Americans were treated this way. When the war ended in 1945, they were allowed to leave the camps.

MODERN OREGON

For another group, the struggle continued. In the 1950s, Congress closed three Native American reservations in an attempt to mix natives into the general population. However, after mixing in, many natives felt they had lost their identity.

By the late 1960s, Native Americans began organizing their tribes. At the same time, the government began leaving tribal business to the

The Kah-nee-tah Resort in central Oregon is run by the Confederated Tribes of Warm Springs. It offers a golf course, casino, and other recreational activities.

tribes. Today, some Native Americans are thriving because they own profitable gambling casinos. The money earned is used to finance tribal operations. The casinos also benefit the state by attracting tourists.

Tourists have also been attracted to Oregon's clean and beautiful environment. Throughout the years, state leaders enacted laws to protect the environment. Oregon became nationally known for these types of laws during the 1960s and 1970s. In 1969, Oregon established the Department of Environmental Quality (DEQ), which protects Oregon's water and air quality, regulates noise pollution, and manages the disposal and cleanup of wastes.

However, all situations affecting the environment cannot be controlled. An environmental disaster occurred in 1999 when a ship called the *New Carissa* ran aground in Coos Bay. The ship leaked 70,000 gallons (264,950 liters) of oil into the ocean. Attempts to tow the ship failed. It was finally torpedoed and sunk.

An Intel worker puts on protective gear. Intel develops technology for computers and the Internet.

Although natural resources are still important in Oregon today, the state's economy has become less dependent on them. By the mid-1990s, high-technology industries such as Intel, NEC, Epson, and Hewlett-Packard became an important part of Oregon's manufacturing industry. Other big industries include sportswear, such as Nike, Jantzen, Pendleton Woolen Mills, and Columbia Sportswear.

Another important new industry in Oregon is tourism. Tourism is now one of the state's top sources of income, after wood products and agriculture. Thanks to Oregon's natural beauty, more and more vacationers visit the state each year.

GOVERNING OREGON

Oregon is governed according to its constitution, a document outlining the roles and responsibilities of people involved in the state's government. The constitution also determines the rights of Oregon citizens. The Oregon constitution was written in 1857. Since then, it has been amended, or changed, many times. The constitution can be changed in one of two ways: An Oregon legislator (lawmaker) may suggest a change to the voters, or the voters may sign a written request for a change, known as a petition.

The state's concern with protecting its land and water has led to many environmental protection laws. Oregon was the first state in the nation to pay for bicycle paths with state money. Bicycle paths save fuel and decrease car pollution. The state also led the nation with the first Bottle Bill, which requires money to be refunded, or given back to the customer, when empty beer and soft drink containers are returned to stores. The

Oregon's capitol is the fourth-newest capitol building in the United States.

Bottle Bill has nearly eliminated drink container litter in Oregon and saves natural resources that would be needed to make new containers. It also reduces trash in landfills.

Oregon is well known for involving citizens in government. In 1902, it was the first state to pass a law allowing voters to propose new laws. Before the amendment, only elected officials could suggest laws. Also, all citizens may vote on new laws, instead of only elected officials. The state was also the first in the nation to hand out voter pamphlets, which help to educate voters about the candidates and issues being voted on in elections.

Oregon's citizens are also involved in their government through "home rule." Nine of Oregon's counties are under home rule. This means that these counties are allowed to choose any form of government they wish within certain limits set by the state. Most counties have a group of people called a county commission that manages their affairs. Commissions are made up of three to five elected members. Oregon cities are also run by home rule. Most cities have a council with a manager or mayor in charge.

Oregon's state government has three branches: the executive, legislative, and judicial. The legislative branch makes the laws. The executive branch ensures that Oregon's laws are carried out. The judicial branch interprets, or explains, the laws and determines how to punish lawbreakers.

LEGISLATIVE BRANCH

Two groups make up the legislative branch. The first group is the house of representatives, which has sixty members. Each member is elected for two years. The second group is the senate, which has thirty members. Each senator is elected for four years. The house and the senate meet in January of each odd-numbered year. In between those scheduled meetings, special committees work on laws.

A bill is a proposed, or suggested, law. A bill can start in the house of representatives or the senate. Voters can also suggest bills by submitting signed petitions. All bills must be voted on in the house of representatives and the senate. A majority of the votes in both houses and a *yes* vote from the governor are needed before a bill can become a law. If the governor vetoes (rejects) a bill, it can still become law if two in three votes in both houses are in favor of the bill.

The senate chambers are inside the capitol.

EXECUTIVE BRANCH

The executive branch is responsible for making sure the state's laws are carried out. The governor is head of the executive branch. The people of Oregon elect the governor to no more than two four-year terms in one twelve-year period. He or she supervises the state's budget (a guide for how money will be spent) and plans for Oregon's future. The governor also helps the state's agencies, boards, and committees, which are also part of the executive branch, to work together. These agencies include the education department, the department of agriculture, and the department of environmental quality, among other things.

Other members of the executive branch include the secretary of state, state treasurer, attorney general, commissioner of labor and industries, and superintendent of public instruction. Oregon voters elect these members of the executive branch, including the governor, every four years.

JUDICIAL BRANCH

The judicial branch determines if someone has broken a state law and decides his or her punishment. It also resolves legal disagreements between two or more parties. These jobs are carried out through the court system.

Oregon's most important court is the state supreme court. Seven justices (judges) are elected to six-year terms on the supreme court. One of these is a chief justice, who is elected by the group. Supreme court judges mostly handle appeals. When someone believes a court has made an unfair decision about his or her case, he or she may make an appeal or request for review, to an appellate court, which reviews decisions of the lower courts. The supreme court and the court of appeals are Oregon's appellate courts.

OREGON STATE GOVERNMENT

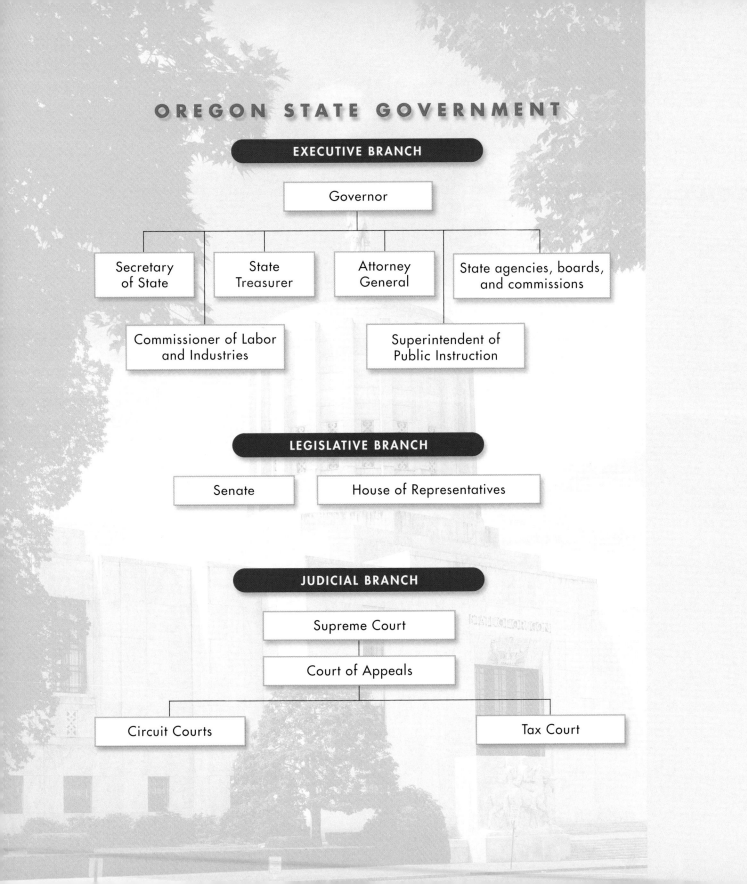

EXECUTIVE BRANCH

Governor

Secretary of State

State Treasurer

Attorney General

State agencies, boards, and commissions

Commissioner of Labor and Industries

Superintendent of Public Instruction

LEGISLATIVE BRANCH

Senate

House of Representatives

JUDICIAL BRANCH

Supreme Court

Court of Appeals

Circuit Courts

Tax Court

OREGON GOVERNORS

Name	Term	Name	Term
Whiteaker, John	1859–1862	Norblad, A. W.	1929–1931
Gibbs, A. C.	1862–1866	Meier, Julius L.	1931–1935
Woods, George L.	1866–1870	Martin, Charles H.	1935–1939
Grover, LaFayette	1870–1877	Sprague, Charles A.	1939–1943
Chadwick, Stephen F.	1877–1878	Snell, Earl	1943–1947
Thayer, W. W.	1878–1882	Hall, John H.	1947–1949
Moody, Z. F.	1882–1887	McKay, Douglas	1949–1952
Pennoyer, Sylvester	1887–1895	Patterson, Paul L.	1952–1956
Lord, William Paine	1895–1899	Smith, Elmo	1956–1957
Geer, T. T.	1899–1903	Holmes, Robert D.	1957–1959
Chamberlain, George E.	1903–1909	Hatfield, Mark O.	1959–1967
Benson, Frank W.	1909–1910	McCall, Tom	1967–1975
Bowerman, Jay	1910–1911	Straub, Robert W.	1975–1979
West, Oswald	1911–1915	Atiyeh, Victor G.	1979–1987
Withycombe, James	1915–1919	Goldschmidt, Neil	1987–1991
Olcott, Ben W.	1919–1923	Roberts, Barbara	1991–1995
Pierce, Walter M.	1923–1927	Kitzhaber, John A.	1995–2003
Patterson, I. L.	1927–1929	Kulongoski, Ted	2003–

Six judges serve on Oregon's court of appeals. The court of appeals oversees civil and criminal appeals. A civil case resolves legal problems between two individuals. A criminal case is brought against a person who has broken the law. For example, robbery is a criminal act.

The Oregon tax court deals with questions about state tax laws. A tax is money paid to support the government. There are also thirty-six circuit courts. Circuit courts are general trial courts and hear all kinds of cases. In civil cases, a circuit court can grant divorces, approve adoptions, and find foster care for children, among other things. In criminal cases, circuit courts decide a person's guilt or innocence, and determine punishment for breaking the law.

Built in the 1860s, Portland's Pioneer Courthouse was the first courthouse on the West Coast.

> ### TAKE A TOUR OF SALEM, OREGON'S STATE CAPITAL

Jason Lee, a Methodist missionary, founded Salem in 1840. It was the first American settlement in the Willamette Valley, but it grew slowly. In the 1840s, almost half the population left the area to mine for gold in California.

Today, Salem's population is nearly 137,000. It is Oregon's third largest city, located 47 miles (76 km) south of Portland. The Oregon State Fair takes place in Salem each year.

The statue on top of the capitol building was originally called "Oregon Pioneer" by its creator, Ulric H. Ellerhusen.

Salem is the center of Oregon's government. The capitol building was built in 1938 after the original one burned down. The building is dome-topped, with a 23-foot- (7-m-) golden pioneer symbolizing Oregon's settlers perched at the top. Inside you'll find art and historical exhibits, as well as the governor's office. You can tour the building or step onto the observation deck to view the city.

Salem places worth seeing include Mission Mill Village, a group of restored historic buildings. One is the Thomas Kay Woolen Mill, built in 1889. At that time, it was one of several woolen mills operating in the Willamette Valley. In the mill, you can see exhibits showing each stage of the wool-making process.

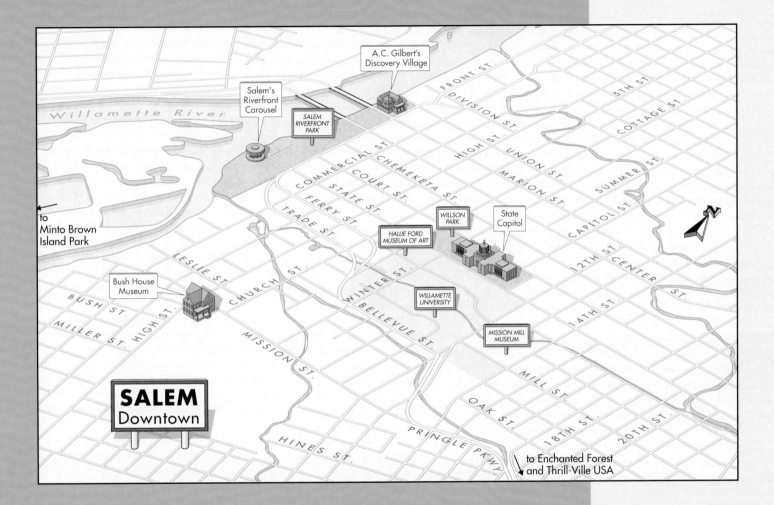

A.C. Gilbert's
Discovery Village

Salem's
Riverfront
Carousel

SALEM
RIVERFRONT
PARK

Willamette River

to
Minto Brown
Island Park

FRONT ST.

DIVISION ST.

5TH ST.

COTTAGE ST.

HIGH ST.

UNION ST.

MARION ST.

SUMMER ST.

COMMERCIAL ST.

CHEMEKETA ST.

COURT ST.

STATE ST.

FERRY ST.

TRADE ST.

HALLIE FORD
MUSEUM OF ART

WILLSON
PARK

State
Capitol

CAPITOL ST.

12TH ST.

CENTER ST.

LESLIE ST.

CHURCH ST.

WINTER ST.

BELLEVUE ST.

WILLAMETTE
UNIVERSITY

14TH ST.

Bush House
Museum

BUSH ST.

HIGH ST.

MILLER ST.

MISSION ST.

MISSION MILL
MUSEUM

MILL ST.

OAK ST.

18TH ST.

20TH ST.

SALEM
Downtown

HINES ST.

PRINGLE PKWY.

to Enchanted Forest
and Thrill-Ville USA

(opposite)
Founded in 1889, the
Thomas Kay Woolen
Mill once produced fine
woolen blankets and
fabrics.

Another interesting historic site is Bush House, a large Victorian home built by businessman Asahel Bush II in 1878. As founder of the *Oregon Statesman* newspaper and Ladd & Bush Bank, Bush was one of the most distinguished people in Oregon history. Much of his home remains as it once was; you can view furniture and wallpaper unchanged since 1878.

If you like art, stop by the Hallie Ford Museum of Art. As part of Willamette University, it is the second largest art museum in the state. It has more than seventy Native American baskets and art from the Northwest, Europe, and Asia.

Another interesting place to visit is A. C. Gilbert Discovery Village, which honors the inventor of the Erector Set, A. C. Gilbert. Check out the 53-foot- (16-m-) tall Erector Set tower. There are two Victorian houses with exhibits and a large outdoor play area.

When you're ready for some fresh air, there are 899 acres (364 ha) to explore at Minto-Brown Island Park. Check out the play structure or explore the wild areas. Bring a picnic, or jog the walking trails.

Take a ride on the brilliantly colored horses of Salem's Riverfront Carousel. The people of Salem donated money, carved horses, and volunteered time in order to set the horses trotting around their carousel. The carousel is open from May through September.

The Enchanted Forest, south of Salem, is an amusement park for kids. The Enchanted Forest has a Storybook Land, an English Village, a mining town, a haunted house, a bobsled run, rides, and a theater. Right beside the Enchanted Forest is another amusement park called Thrill-Ville USA, with a roller coaster and other rides.

WHO'S WHO IN OREGON?

A. C. Gilbert (1884–1962) is known as "the man who saved Christmas." During World War I, the United States Congress wanted to turn Gilbert's Connecticut toy factory into a weapons and ammunition factory. To save the factory, Gilbert took his Erector Sets to Congress and argued that children's play was as important as fighting the war because it helped young people to learn. Congress agreed to leave his factory for making toys. Gilbert was born in Salem.

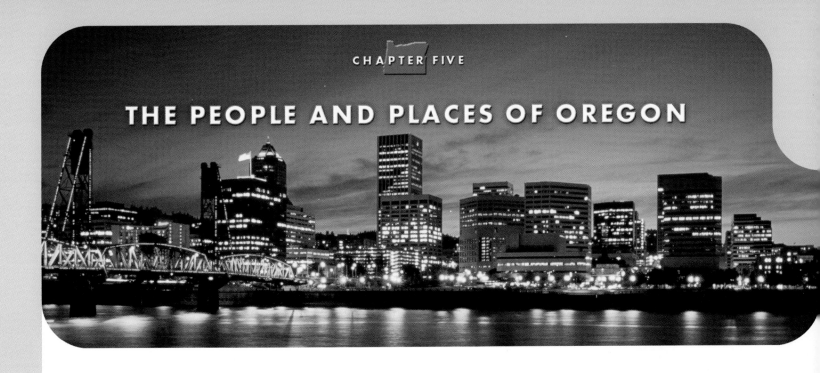

CHAPTER FIVE

THE PEOPLE AND PLACES OF OREGON

In 2001, approximately 3,471,700 people lived in Oregon. Between 1980 and 1998, Oregon's population increased by almost one-fourth. Experts predict that Oregon will continue to grow faster than the country as a whole over the next fifty years. Some of the reasons people move to Oregon are the low cost of living, recreational opportunities (such as fishing, skiing, and boating), nice retirement areas, and plentiful job opportunities.

According to the 2000 Census, 87 in every 100 Oregonians are of European descent. The state's Hispanic population (people from a Spanish-speaking country) has been growing rapidly in recent years. While only 4 in 100 people were Hispanic in 1990, 8 in 100 were Hispanic in 2000. Other groups in Oregon include African-Americans (almost 2 in 100), Asian Americans (3 in 100), and Native Americans (1 in 100). Other ethnic groups account for fewer than 1 in 100 people in the state.

With more than 500,000 residents, Portland has been called the best big city in North America.

Most of Oregon's population is in the northwest. The Willamette Valley is the most densely populated area of Oregon. In 2000, about 1 in 6 people, or 529,121 people, lived in Portland. Eugene was the next largest city, with 137,893 people. The state's capital, Salem, was in third place with 136,924 people.

WORKING IN OREGON

Timber is Oregon's top industry. Oregon's forests produce more timber than any other state. But environmental concerns and disappearing forests have resulted in fewer timber-related jobs (such as logging, lumber millwork, and lumber truck drivers). High-technology jobs and service jobs such as health care or business services are becoming more common. The manufacture of electronics (such as computer parts, software, and measurement devices) is also growing quickly.

Agriculture is another important industry. Most of the state's 40,000 farms are small and family owned. In 2001, Oregon's agricultural production totaled $3.7 billion and provided about 140,000 jobs. There are more than 200 agricultural products from Oregon. The state leads the nation in the production of Christmas trees, grass seed, berries, peppermint, and hazelnuts. Its farms also produce potatoes, pears, greenhouse and nursery products (plants), hay, beef, and wheat.

A helicopter irrigates a Christmas tree farm in Oregon.

There are several agricultural regions in Oregon. The Willamette Valley grows vegetables, berries, hazelnuts, hops, and nursery products. In southern Oregon, farmers grow fruits, potatoes, and livestock. Dairy farms and fisheries are found at the coast. The Columbia Basin grows wheat, fruit, and livestock. In eastern Oregon, farmers grow onions, potatoes, and sugar beets. Southeastern Oregon specializes in livestock and hay. Parts of central Oregon, such as Jefferson County, produce seeds, peppermint, grains, livestock, and hay.

Mining employs about 2,000 workers. There are more than 400 mines in the state. Mining produces clay, gemstones, sand, gravel, stone, and gold.

Manufacturing in Oregon was once tied mainly to the timber industry. Now manufacturing covers a variety of industries. Most manufacturers are located in or near large cities such as Portland, although some are found in less-populated areas such as southern and eastern Oregon. Oregon's main manufacturing businesses are forest products (such as paper and plywood), high technology (such as computers and electronic equipment), food, and metals.

Tourism is one of Oregon's main industries, thanks to the many visitors who want to enjoy the state's natural beauty. Tourists play, sightsee, and relax in Oregon's deserts, rivers, mountains, and valleys. In 1999, tourists spent more than $5 billion in Oregon. About 80,000 Oregonians work in tourism-related jobs, including managing hotels or motels, leading tours, and guiding boats down rivers. Some of the state's most popular sites include the Columbia River Gorge, the Cascade Range, Crater Lake National Park, and historic sites.

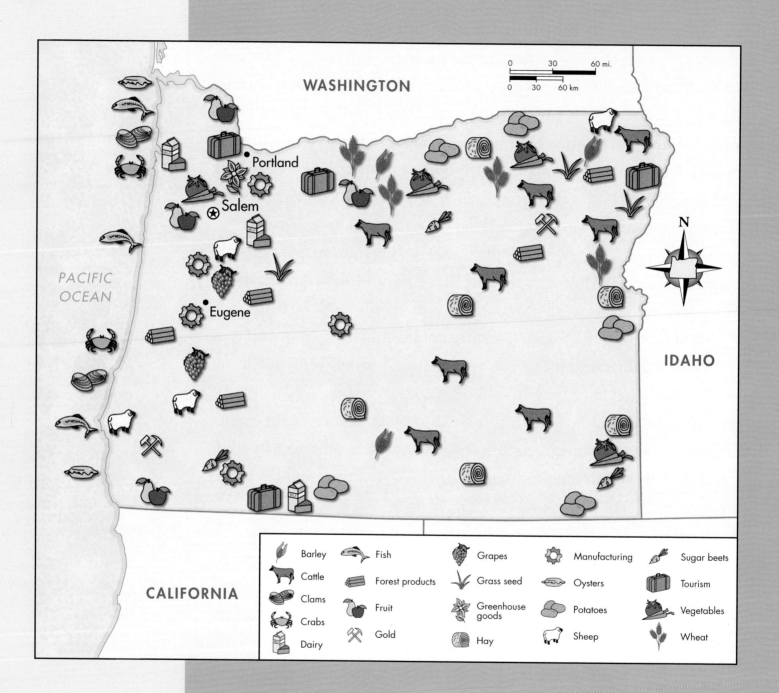

WASHINGTON

Portland

Salem

PACIFIC
OCEAN

Eugene

IDAHO

N

CALIFORNIA

	Barley		Fish		Grapes		Manufacturing		Sugar beets
	Cattle		Forest products		Grass seed		Oysters		Tourism
	Clams		Fruit		Greenhouse goods		Potatoes		Vegetables
	Crabs		Gold		Hay		Sheep		Wheat
	Dairy								

Eastern Oregon is famous for its potatoes (sometimes called "spuds"). In fact, McDonald's gets most of its potatoes for French fries from eastern Oregon! The Tillamook area in western Oregon is well known for dairy products. Put them together and you have scrumptious stuffed spuds. Don't forget to ask an adult for help.

STUFFED SPUDS

4 large baking potatoes
4 tablespoons butter
1/2 cup milk
1 cup shredded cheddar cheese
salt
pepper
paprika

1. Scrub potatoes. Prick each potato several times with a fork.
2. Bake uncovered in a 400° oven for 1 hour.
3. Carefully remove potatoes using potholders. Cut a thick slice from the top of each potato.
4. Use a big spoon to carefully scoop the white potato pulp from the skin, leaving shells about 1/2 inch thick.
5. Use an electric mixer to beat the potato innards until smooth. Add cheese, butter, and milk. Beat with mixer to combine. Add salt and pepper to taste.
6. Spoon mixture evenly into potato skin shells.
7. Place stuffed potatoes on a rimmed baking sheet. Sprinkle lightly with paprika.
8. Bake uncovered in a 375° oven for 20 to 30 minutes. Potato tops should be golden brown. Makes 4 servings.

Northeastern Oregon

Let's begin our tour in northeastern Oregon. Towns in this region are small and remote. You may spot cowboys, wheat farms, and ranches. You'll see the Blue and Wallowa Mountains, where you can fish, swim, or boat. You can also hike through a ghost town.

The Tamástslikt Cultural Institute is just east of Pendleton. The museum shows how the Oregon Trail changed the lives of Native Americans. You'll see Indian-made tools and clothes, watch films, and see exhibits showing what life was like before and after non-native settlers arrived. The museum is part of the Confederated Tribes of the Umatilla Indian Reservation.

More Oregon Trail history can be seen at a museum in Baker City—the Oregon Trail Interpretive Park. There are video clips and photos of the largest overland migration in Northern America. You'll hear voices reading the pioneers' diary entries and see a life-size wagon-train scene. Outside, a trail leads to the ruts from the settlers' wagons, at the end of their journey west.

If you want to see North America's deepest gorge, head for Hells Canyon. Because of the rugged area, you can reach parts of Hells Canyon only by boat, horse, or on foot. The few roads are rough; you'll need a four-wheel-drive vehicle. Or, get a different perspective of the canyon by whitewater rafting or riding in a jet boat on the wild and scenic Snake River.

Central Oregon

There's plenty of outdoor recreation in central Oregon. Unlike western Oregon, the sun shines three hundred days per year. You can hike, fish, ski, camp, mountain-bike, or raft. View the forests and volcanoes of the western and high Cascades. To the south, there's range country and wetlands. Oregon's only national park, Crater Lake, is in this area.

There are many beautiful sights, such as the rich farms of the Willamette Valley, the Columbia River Gorge waterfalls, and lava flows near Bend. The 11,235-foot (3,427-m) Mount Hood is also impressive. Backpackers love the Three Sisters Wilderness, near a town called Sisters.

At the Museum at Warm Springs, learn about the history of the Confederated Tribes of the Warm Springs Reservation, including the Wasco, Warm Springs, and Paiute tribes. The museum holds various types of traditional houses and displays of many Native American objects. These include baskets, beadwork, and other artwork as well as exhibits about fishing and root gathering.

Climbers approach the peak of Mount Hood, one of the most frequently climbed glaciated mountains in the world.

61

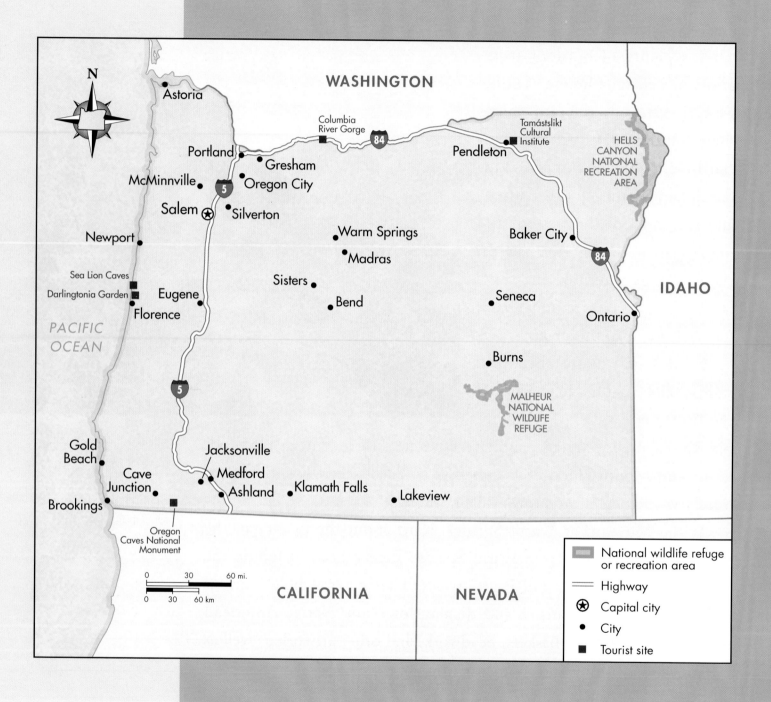

N

WASHINGTON

Astoria

Columbia
River Gorge
84

Tamástslikt
Cultural
Institute

HELLS
CANYON
NATIONAL
RECREATION
AREA

Portland
Gresham

Pendleton

McMinnville
5
Oregon City

Salem ⊛ Silverton

Baker City

Newport

Warm Springs

84

Madras

IDAHO

Sea Lion Caves

Sisters

Darlingtonia Garden
Eugene

Bend

Seneca

Florence

Ontario

PACIFIC
OCEAN

Burns

MALHEUR
NATIONAL
WILDLIFE
REFUGE

Gold
Beach

Jacksonville

Cave
Junction

Medford
Ashland

Klamath Falls

Lakeview

Brookings

Oregon
Caves National
Monument

0   30   60 mi.

0   30   60 km

CALIFORNIA

NEVADA

National wildlife refuge
or recreation area

Highway

⊛ Capital city

● City

■ Tourist site

Southeastern Oregon

The southeastern corner of the state is flat and dry. Not many people live in this area. Those who do live there make a living by cattle ranching. At the town of Lakeview, there's an old resort with a natural hot springs called Hunter's Hot Springs. Lakeview is also the site of the only active geyser (a spring that periodically shoots boiling water and steam into the air) in the far west. The geyser is called Old Perpetua. It sometimes shoots water more than 50 feet (15 m) into the air!

The Malheur National Wildlife Refuge is south of Burns. You'll see birds such as swans, egrets, herons, golden eagles, and hawks. Some bird-watchers claim to have seen more than one hundred types of birds there in one day.

FIND OUT MORE

The name Old Perpetua is based on the word *perpetual*. Look up *perpetual* in the dictionary and find out why Perpetua might not be the best name for this geyser!

A pair of cinnamon teal ducks make themselves at home at Malheur National Wildlife Refuge.

Southern Oregon

In southern Oregon, stop by Klamath Falls to see the Favell Museum of Western Art and Indian Artifacts, one of the nation's best museums of cowboy art. You'll also see displays of native objects including arrowheads, baskets, pottery, and other items. Another Klamath City museum for Native American artifacts is Klamath County Museum. The Klamath Indians are based in Chiloquin, north of Upper Klamath Lake.

The marble cave at Oregon Caves National Monument was formed over hundreds of thousands of years.

EXTRA! EXTRA!

Stalactites and stalagmites are icicle-shaped rocks found within caves. Stalactites hang down from a cave's ceiling, while stalagmites stick up from the ground. One way to remember the difference: *stalactite* has a c in it, for "ceiling." *Stalagmite* has a g in it, for "ground." Sometimes a stalactite and stalagmite join together and form a *column*.

Nearby Jacksonville has been restored to look like its gold-boom days. Jacksonville also hosts the Britt Festivals between mid-June and early September, where well known performers give musical and theatrical shows on an outdoor stage.

The Oregon Caves, near the town of Cave Junction, are worth a visit. You'll see room-sized caverns, stalactites and stalagmites, and other interesting formations. Bring a jacket, even in summer—the caves are cool in more ways than one!

The Coast

Oregonians are proud that their beaches are public. Anyone, anytime, can enjoy Oregon's coastline, unlike some states where private citizens can own the beaches and may choose not to allow others to use them. The Pacific Ocean is chilly even on warm days. Some people surf or windsurf, but they have to wear a thick wetsuit because the water is so cold. There are lots of other things to do, such as flying kites and watching sea creatures and plants in tide pools.

At Gold Beach, just north of Brookings, jet boats zoom up and down the Rogue River. Passengers will get sprayed with water as the boat turns. A guide discusses the history of the river and points out interesting plants and other river features. You may spot bears, otters, ospreys, and other wildlife.

If you drive along the Oregon coast during winter or spring, watch for whales spouting in the ocean. You may see signs along the road that say "Whale Watching Spoken Here." At these places, volunteers who are knowledgeable about whales point out any whales in the area and discuss them.

Want to see some man-eating plants? They don't actually eat people. The plants are carnivorous (meat eaters) but they only eat bugs. The bug-eating greenery grows at Darlingtonia Garden, 4 miles (6.4 km) north of Florence.

You can check out some sea lions at the Sea Lion Caves between Florence and Newport. An elevator ride takes you down into the world's largest sea cave. The cave is as tall as a stack of twelve houses, and as long as a football field. Sea lions live in the cave during the fall and winter, and outside on the rocks the rest of the year. They are incredibly noisy, but fun to watch.

The Kite Festival is an annual event in the coastal town of Lincoln City.

Sea lions lie on the rocks at Sea Lion Caves, the largest sea lion cave in the world.

At Fort Clatsop National Memorial, costumed actors demonstrate what life was like in the early 1800s.

Stop at the Oregon Coast Museum in Newport. Stroll through the clear plastic tunnel, while live sharks and skates swim around you. Watch otters play, and view the many wondrous exhibits of sea life.

In Astoria, visit Fort Clatsop National Memorial. The wooden fort is a reconstruction of Lewis and Clark's camp in the winter of 1805–1806. Another unique attraction is the Astoria Column, built in 1926. It was patterned after a column in Rome and stands 125 feet (38 m) tall. You can climb up inside and look far into the distance, or just look at the historical murals (paintings) on the outside walls.

Portland Area

Portland, Oregon's largest city, lies where the Willamette and Columbia rivers meet. The surroundings are amazing. You only need to drive a short way to walk the beach, view a waterfall, ski, or hike Mount Hood. You can also find a patch of wilderness within Portland called Forest Park. Some people have seen deer and coyotes there.

EXTRA! EXTRA!

Portland's Mill Ends Park, just 2 feet (0.6 meters) in diameter, is the world's smallest park. A man named Dick Fagan once worked at a newspaper office above where the park now stands. Every day he looked at a small weedy spot outside his office until one day, when he decided to plant flowers there. He named the spot Mill Ends Park, after the name of his newspaper column. Fagan described the park in his column and told stories of leprechauns living there.

Portland is famous for its beautiful flowers, especially roses. Police cars have roses on their doors. You can visit the International Rose Test Gardens to see and smell thousands of rose bushes. The city has many parks and gardens, including an interesting Japanese garden.

If you enjoy museums, you'll love Portland. At the Portland Art Museum, you can view Northwest Coast Native American collections, artwork by Northwest artists, and other exhibits. The Oregon History Center honors Oregon's past, from before the arrival of the first European explorers up until this century. There you'll see a covered wagon, native artifacts, ocean-going instruments, and modern objects.

Experience earthquakes and tornadoes at the Oregon Museum of Science and Industry, where you can also tour a submarine and play with many hands-on exhibits. Learn about trees and forest resources at the World Forestry Center. At Portland Children's Museum, make clay sculptures, blow enormous bubbles, and enjoy other fun activities.

When you've seen enough Portland museums, you may want to take a tour of the city. You can take a walking tour to see fountains, parks, art, and historic places. Bus tours stop at various museums, parks, and waterfalls in the Columbia Gorge. One bus tour includes a trip on a riverboat.

Science means fun at the Oregon Museum of Science and Industry, where you can take part in interactive exhibits and hands-on demonstrations.

Visitors can get a close-up view of Multnomah Falls from Benson Bridge.

Statues of a famous children's author, Beverly Cleary, and the characters in her books are located at the Beverly Cleary Sculpture Garden in northeast Portland. If you've read Ms. Cleary's books about Ramona Quimby or Henry Huggins, you might want to see the Ramona, Henry, and Ribsy (Henry's dog) sculptures. You can also splash around in the water fountains.

Next, drive through the Columbia Gorge to view cliffs, waterfalls, ferns, and spring wildflowers. One of the most popular destinations in the gorge is Multnomah Falls. You can hike to the top of the falls, which drops 620 feet (189 m).

Willamette Valley

Meadows and forests lie between Portland and Eugene. This valley is what the Oregon Trail pioneers dreamed about. Fields of berries, hops, grass seed, Christmas trees, grapes, hazelnuts, and irises grow in the area's rich soil. Throughout much of the year, you can sample the region's produce at farms and fruit stands.

In Oregon City, visit the End of the Oregon Trail Interpretive Center. Costumed guides lead you through three huge wagons of displays. Another interesting Oregon City spot is the McLoughlin House where kindhearted John McLoughlin retired. The Clackamas County Historical Society Museum displays old diaries, photos, pioneer and Native American artifacts, and a horse-drawn carriage. Just south of town, stop to view Willamette Falls, the largest waterfall in the west at 40 feet (12 m) high and 1,300 feet (396 m) wide.

If you love airplanes, you'll want to visit the Evergreen Aviation Museum in McMinnville. There you can see "The Spruce Goose," a famous cargo-type flying boat, and many other aircraft. You'll also hear talks and view exhibits on flying and airplanes. More aviation exhibits can be found in Eugene at the Oregon Air and Space Museum. Examine the museum's old planes and jets to learn about the history of aviation in Oregon.

With its beautiful scenery, historical significance, and cultural attractions, it's no wonder that Oregon continues to attract people even today. Welcome to Oregon country!

The covered wagon-shaped building at the End of the Oregon Trail Interpretive Center features exhibits and presentations about the Oregon Trail.

OREGON ALMANAC

Statehood date and number: February 14, 1859; 33rd

State seal: A shield supported by thirty-three stars, divided by a ribbon with the words "the Union." Above the ribbon are mountains, forest, an elk, a covered wagon, the Pacific Ocean with a setting sun, and a departing British ship. Below the ribbon are a plow, a pickax, and a clump of wheat. The American eagle is the crest. Around the outside of the seal is the phrase, "State of Oregon 1859." Adopted in 1903.

State flag: Navy blue with gold lettering and symbols. Above a shield surrounded by thirty-three stars are the words, "State of Oregon." Below the shield is "1859." A beaver is displayed on the back of the flag. Adopted in 1925.

Geographic center: Crook, 25 miles (40 km) south-southeast of Prineville

Total area/rank: 97,131 square miles (251,568 sq km)/10th

Coastline: 362 miles (582 km)

Borders: Washington, Idaho, Nevada, California, Pacific Ocean

Latitude and longitude: Oregon is located approximately between 42° and 46° 18' N and 116° 28' and 124° 34' W.

Highest/lowest elevation: Mount Hood, 11,239 feet (3,426 m)/Pacific Ocean, sea level

Hottest/coldest temperature: 119° F (48° C) on August 10, 1898, in Pendleton/–54° F (–48° C) on February 10, 1933, in Seneca

Land area/rank: 96,002 square miles (248,645 sq km)/10th

Inland water area/rank: 1,129 square miles (2,924 sq km)/19th

Population (2000 Census)/rank: 3,421,399/28th

Population of major cities:

Portland: 529,121

Eugene: 137,893

Salem: 136,924

Origin of state name: Possibly named for the Columbia River, once called the Oregon or *Ouragan* (French for *hurricane*)

State capital: Salem (since 1855)

Previous capitals: Moved from Oregon City to Salem in 1851, to Corvallis in 1855, and back to Salem in 1855

Counties: 36

State government: 60 representatives, 30 senators

Major rivers/lakes: Columbia, Snake, Willamette, John Day/Upper Klamath Lake, Malheur Lake, Crater Lake

Farm products: Christmas trees, hazelnuts, grass seed, peppermint, raspberries, blackberries, loganberries, marionberries, hops, strawberries, prunes, plums, onions, cauliflower, pears, nursery products, hay, wheat, corn

Livestock: Cattle, sheep

Manufactured products: High-technology electronics (microcomputer chips, printers, test and measurement equipment, software); forest products (lumber, wood products, paper, plywood, manufactured homes); metals (aluminum, steel, tools, hardware); transportation equipment (travel trailers, motor coaches, boats, airplanes, train cars); food processing (canned and frozen vegetables and fruits, bread, fish, packaged meats, sausages, prepared meats, milk, cheese, nuts, wine and beer, soft drinks)

Mining products: Sand, gravel, crushed rock

Fishing products: Salmon, snapper, sole, sablefish, Pacific whiting, Dungeness crab, pink shrimp, albacore tuna

Animal: American beaver

Bird: Western meadowlark

Fish: Chinook salmon

Flower: Oregon grape

Gem: Oregon sunstone

Insect: Oregon swallowtail butterfly

Motto: "She Flies with Her Own Wings"

Nickname: Beaver State

Nut: Hazelnut

Rock: Thunder-egg (geode)

Seashell: Oregon hairy triton

Song: "Oregon, My Oregon," written by J. A. Buchanan and Henry B. Murtagh

Tree: Douglas fir

Wildlife: Deer, elk, antelopes, foxes, waterfowls, gray whales, sea lions, harbor seals, salmon, bald eagles, beavers, cougars, bears, bighorn sheep

TIME**LINE**

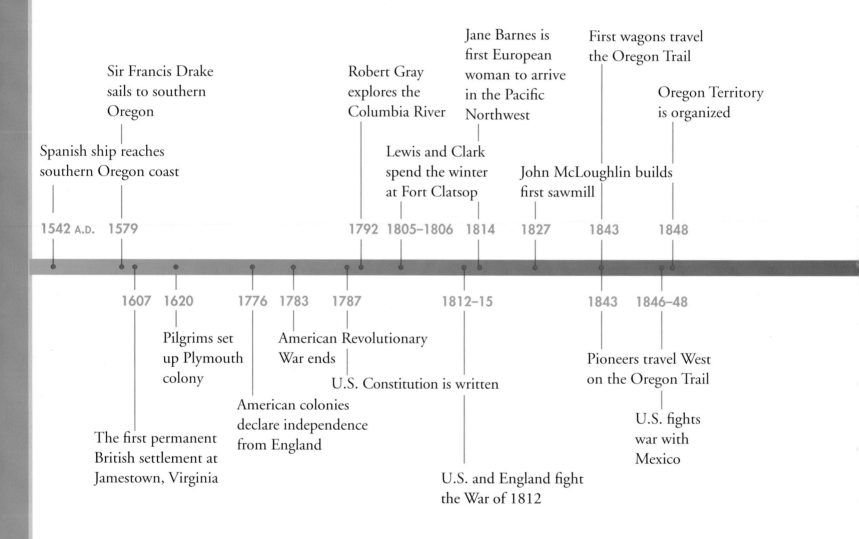

Sir Francis Drake
sails to southern
Oregon

Robert Gray
explores the
Columbia River

Jane Barnes is
first European
woman to arrive
in the Pacific
Northwest

First wagons travel
the Oregon Trail

Oregon Territory
is organized

Spanish ship reaches
southern Oregon coast

Lewis and Clark
spend the winter
at Fort Clatsop

John McLoughlin builds
first sawmill

1542 A.D.   1579   1792 1805–1806 1814   1827   1843   1848

         1607 1620   1776 1783 1787   1812–15   1843 1846–48

Pilgrims set
up Plymouth
colony

American Revolutionary
War ends

Pioneers travel West
on the Oregon Trail

U.S. Constitution is written

U.S. fights
war with
Mexico

American colonies
declare independence
from England

The first permanent
British settlement at
Jamestown, Virginia

U.S. and England fight
the War of 1812

America's first policewoman,
Lola Greene Baldwin, joins
Portland force

Oregon's first children's school
is started; gold is discovered in
southern Oregon

Portland's Kaiser Shipyards
becomes world's biggest
shipbuilder

Freighter *New
Carissa* runs
aground off
Coos Bay

Congress ratifies Oregon
State constitution

Nation's first bottle
bill is approved

| 1851 | 1859 | 1908 | 1940 | 1971 | 1999 |

| 1861–65 | 1917–18 | 1929 | 1941–45 | 1950–53 | 1964 | 1965–73 | 1969 | 1991 | 1995 |

U.S. takes part in
World War I

Civil rights laws
passed in the U.S.

U.S. and other nations
fight in Persian Gulf War

U.S. fights in
World War II

U.S. fights in the
Vietnam War

The stock market
crashes and U.S.
enters the Great
Depression

U.S. fights in the
Korean War

U.S. space shuttle
docks with Russian
space station

Civil War
occurs in the
United States

Neil Armstrong
and Edwin
Aldrin land on
the moon

GALLERY OF FAMOUS OREGONIANS

James Beard

(1903–1985)

A chef known as the Father of American Cooking because his cookbooks and magazine articles paid tribute to American cooking. Born in Portland.

Beverly Cleary

(1916–)

Award-winning writer of children's books, including stories about Ramona Quimby set in Portland. Her books include *Ramona the Brave, Ramona the Pest,* and *Beezus and Ramona.* Born in McMinnville.

Jan Eliot

(1950–)

Cartoonist and creator of the newspaper comic strip "Stone Soup." Lives in Eugene.

Matt Groening

(1954–)

Cartoonist and creator of *The Simpsons.* Born in Portland.

Ken Kesey

(1935–2001)

Well-known author. One of his novels, *Sometime a Great Notion,* was also made into a movie and is a story about Oregon loggers. Lived in Springfield.

Philip Knight

(1938–)

Co-founder of Nike, one of the world's largest sports companies and headquartered in Beaverton. Born in Portland.

Ursula K. LeGuin

(1929–)

Award-winning author of fantasy and science fiction books. Lives in Portland.

Linus Pauling, Ph.D.

(1901–1994)

Chemist who won two Nobel Prize awards. Considered by many to be one of the greatest scientists of all time. Born in Portland.

Steve Prefontaine

(1951–1975)

Record-breaking track athlete. Born in Coos Bay.

Picabo Street

(1971–)

Won an Olympic gold medal for skiing in 1996. Lives in Portland.

GLOSSARY

alliance: a group formed to serve common interests

ancient: belonging to a time long ago

colony: a group settled in a distant land but still closely tied to its parent country

conservation: carefully using and saving natural resources

constitution: a written system of basic governmental laws

fossil: traces of past plant or animal life that have been preserved in rock

geography: physical features of a place

immigrant: a person who leaves their home country to live in another

industry: business that provides a product or service

population: number of people

reservation: land set aside as a place for Native Americans to live

slavery: the practice of one person owning another person

textile: a woven fabric

tule: a water plant

varied: the introduction of change

volcano: a mountain or hole through which molten rocks, ash, dust, and other materials burst out of the Earth

FOR MORE INFORMATION

Web sites

Oregon.gov
http://www.oregon.gov/
The official web site of Oregon State government.

The Oregon Home Page
http://www.isu.edu/%7Etrinmich/Oregontrail.html
The story of the Oregon trail.

New Perspectives on the West
http://www.pbs.org/weta/thewest/
Information about the people, places, and events of the West from PBS.

Travel Oregon Online
http://www.traveloregon.com/
The official web site of the Oregon Tourism Commission.

Books

Alter, Judy. *Exploring and Mapping the American West.* Danbury, CT: Children's Press, 2001.

Erickson, Paul. *Daily Life in a Covered Wagon.* Glenview, IL: Scott Foresman, 1997.

Freedman, Russell. *Children of the Wild West.* New York, NY: Houghton Mifflin, 1990.

Marsh, Carole. *Oregon History! Surprising Secrets About Our State's Founding Mothers, Fathers & Kids!* Peachtree City, GA: Gallopade, 1996.

Addresses

Oregon Historical Society
1200 S.W. Park Avenue
Portland, OR 97205

State of Oregon
Office of the Governor
254 State Capitol
Salem, OR 97310

INDEX

ABOUT THE AUTHOR

Terry Miller Shannon read dozens of books and took many road trips with her husband, Craig, and her dog, Romeo, to learn about her favorite state. She's thrilled to call Oregon home. Her latest book is *Tub Toys*, a rhyming picture book written with her son. Terry lives in Gold Beach.

Photographs © 2003: AP/Wide World Photos/Jack Smith: 44; Buddy Mays/Travel Stock: 3 right, 17, 68, 71 top left; Corbis Images: 38 (Bettmann), 63 (Darrell Gulin), 51 (Dave G. Houser), 74 left (Murdo MacLeod), 65 bottom (James Marshall), 74 bottom right (Wally McNamee), 74 top right (Roger Ressmeyer), 43 (Tony Roberts), 65 top (Phil Schermeister), 52 left (Joseph Sohm/ChromoSohm Inc.), 28, 39; Dembinsky Photo Assoc.: 71 bottom left (Mike Barlow), 9 (Terry Donnelly), 7 (Scott T. Smith); Hulton|Archive/Getty Images: 23 top; Larry Geddis: 67, 69; MapQuest.com, Inc.: 70 bottom; Nevada Historical Society: 34; North Wind Picture Archives: 20, 21, 25, 29, 30, 32, 35 bottom, 37; Oregon Historical Society: 23 bottom (OrHi646), 26 right (Drawing by Oliver W. Dixon/OrHi1645); Oregon Tourism Division: 70 top; Photo Researchers, NY: 41 (Tim Davis), 64 (Jim Steinberg); Ric Ergenbright: 4, 11, 12, 15; Steve Terrill: cover, 40, 45, 49 background, 71 bottom right; Stock Montage, Inc.: 35 top (The Newberry Library), 19, 22, 24, 26 left, 33, 36; Stone/Getty Images: 56 (Bruce Forster), 61 (Marc Muench), 13 (A & L Sinibaldi), 14 (Greg Vaughn); Superstock, Inc.: 52 right (FourByFive), 3 left, 16, 47, 66; Viesti Collection, Inc./Peter Bennett: 55; Visuals Unlimited/Joe McDonald: 71 top right.